Abrams Books for Young Readers
New York

A *Counting* Book of New York City

JOANNE DUGAN

1 Empire State Building

Climb 1,860 steps to the top of the world's most famous skyscraper.

2 Lions
See them at the library.

3 Black-and-White Cookies

Which side do you like to eat first . . . chocolate or vanilla?

4 Boats

Have a race on the Central Park boat pond.

5 Bridges

They will take you to the big city.

6 *Skyscrapers*

New York has more of them than any other city in the world.

7 Helmets

Stop, drop, and roll!

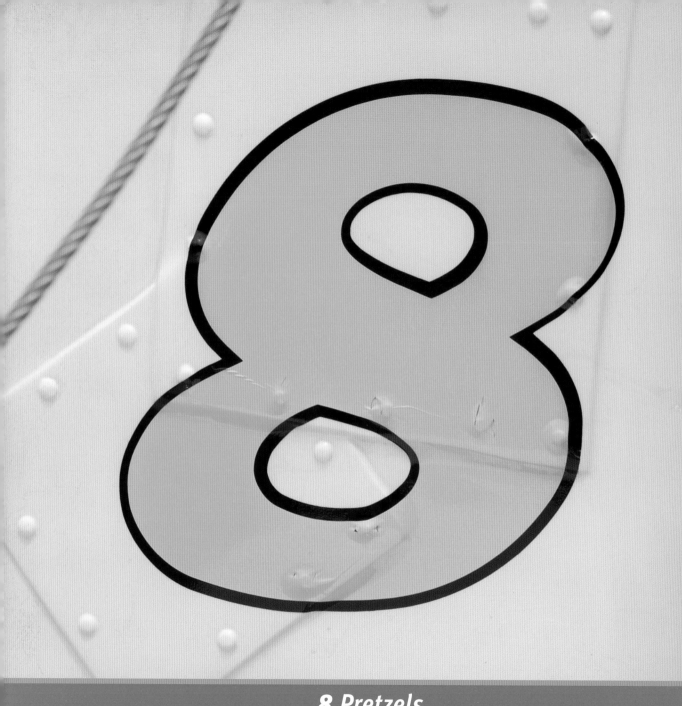

8 Pretzels

Buy one on the street and eat it with mustard.

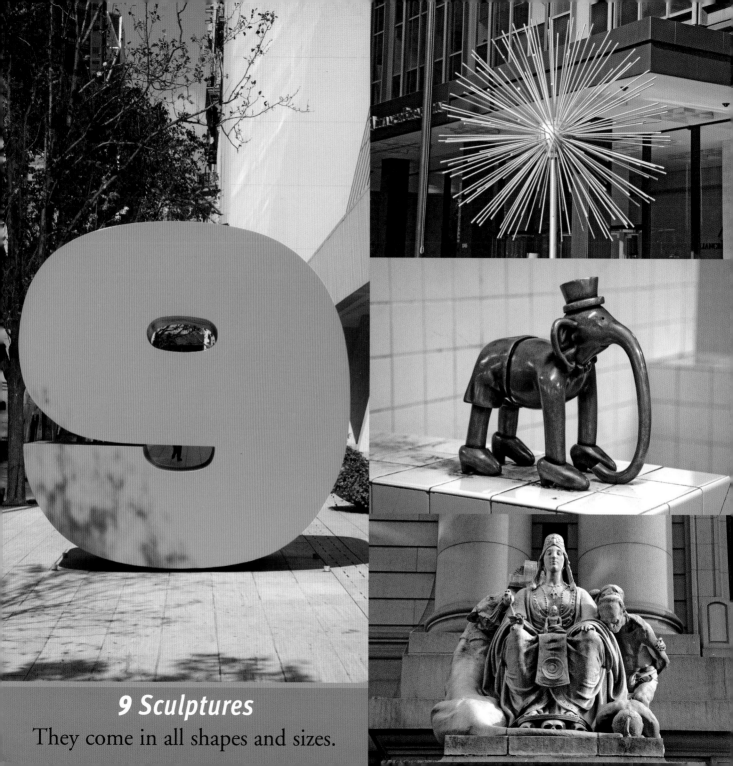

9 Sculptures

They come in all shapes and sizes.

10

10 Shoes

Do you have a favorite?

11 Baseball Gloves

Pick one up and go play ball!

12 Clocks

Count the numbers from one to twelve!

13 Fish

See them on ice in Chinatown.

14 Carousel Horses

Try riding on one with your eyes closed.

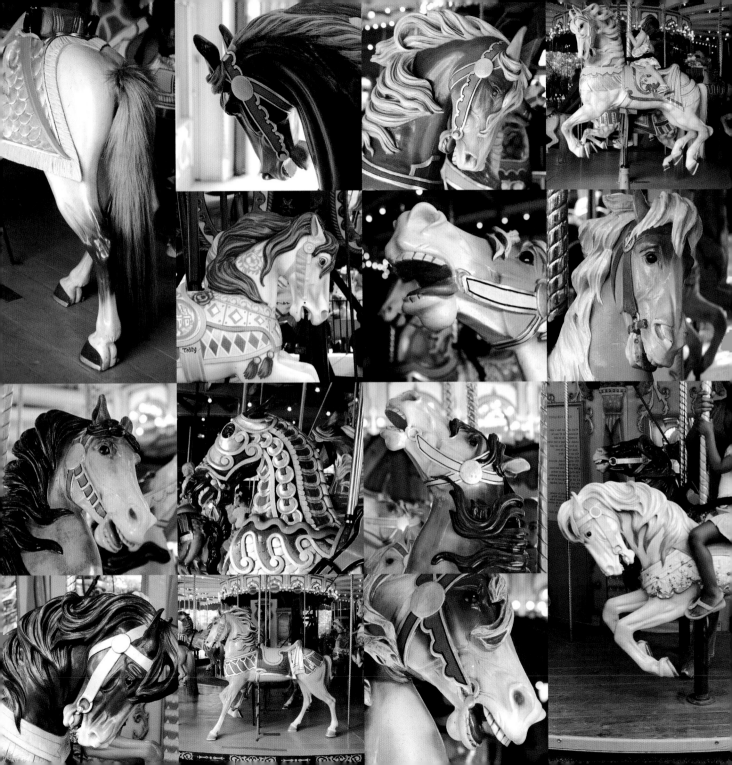

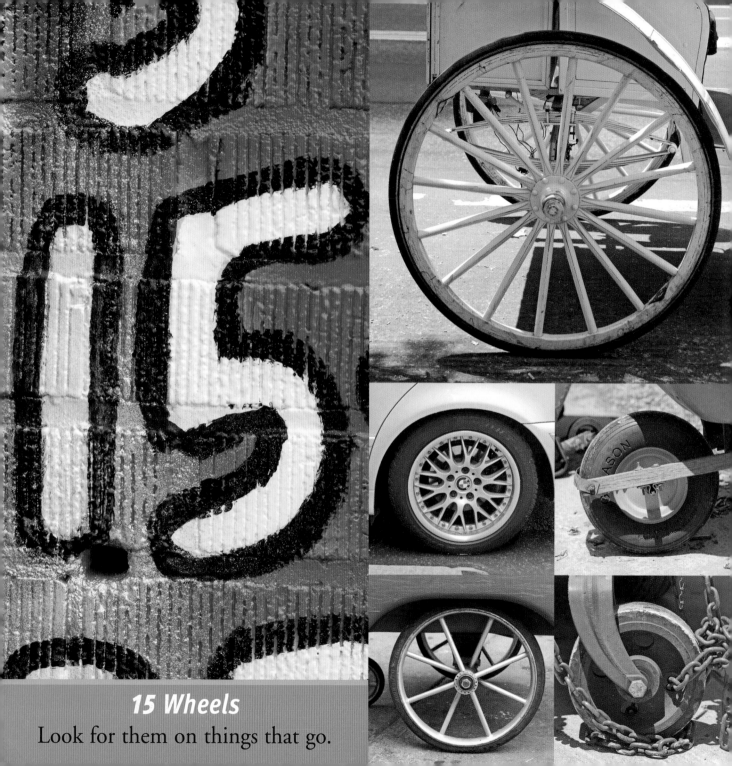

15 Wheels

Look for them on things that go.

16 Arrows
Left or right, up or down, they always point the way.

17 Bagels

Plain, poppy, or pumpernickel?

18 Windows
Look out and enjoy the view.

19

19 Pets

Which one would you like to hold?

20 *Children*

They love New York City!

Where is it?

The idea for *123 NYC: A Counting Book of New York City* came while I was working on *ABC NYC: A Book About Seeing New York City*, the first book of the series. My son, Hugo, and I spent years with a camera, hunting and gathering exotic letterforms from signage and graffiti throughout the five boroughs of New York. We were so happy when this personal journal (first made as a simple teaching tool for a young boy by his photographer mother) became a book to share with kids and adults everywhere.

In the process of making *ABC NYC*, Hugo moved from baby to toddler to talker and became an opinionated expert in all things New York. He pointed out each dog and jackhammer and subway car he saw. Leaving home with him every morning was (and still is) an exercise in seeing the city with fresh eyes and appreciating our urban landscape.

Most things in New York come in quantity. And a book of numbers seemed like the perfect way to collect the amazing range of objects, places, and people of New York. We noticed bagels stacked in street vendor carts, or the many wheels turning on the pavement. The list-making started once again. Hugo and I turned our gaze slightly. And another book began.

123 NYC is designed to inspire the reader to look closely. Whether they are in a city or a small town, I hope this book will encourage kids and adults alike to see their world in a different way and to love the stuff of daily life. Because even my big-city kid (who learned his first numbers from the side of a fire truck) finds something new to marvel at every single day.

Joanne Dugan

Acknowledgments

Biggest thanks to the two loves of my life: Ludovic and Hugo Moulin. Gigantic gratitude to Christine Earle, profound appreciation to Lily McCullough, and big fat thank yous to Howard Reeves, Tamar Brazis, Chad Beckerman, Marie and George Dugan, Annette Dugan, Brett and especially Max Vadset, Clare Brown, Ann Lemon, Jayne Hinds-Bidaut, Jennifer Bezjak, Andrew French, Dennis Costin and Ernie Bynum, Andrew Berger, Anne Alexander and Philip Enny, Nina Kramer and Michael Mojica, Keiko Tase, Dennis Thatchaichawalit, Barbara Aria, Steve White and his Greenwich Village Little League Marlins, Devin Powers at Engine 16, Ladder 7, in Manhattan, Kundalini Yoga East, Paul Fittipaldi, Boris Miller, and everyone at the rental department of Adorama Camera.

A special tap dance of thanks to the subjects who didn't laugh at my crazy and often last-minute requests: Lena and Emmanuel Hobbs-Brown; Vera Thatchaichawalit; Lia Mojica; Thomas, Matthew, and Justine Enny; Taiga Tase; Amos Burkhart; Cynthia and Maurice Black; and the random pedestrians who trustingly allowed me to photograph their shoes, among other things.

Endless appreciation to the very special children of the United Nations International School featured in the last spread of the book—Mohammed, Moris, Cheko, Bennett, Federico, Alexandra, Anna, Lily, Alana, Eyob, Rara, Hugo, Nicky, Remy, Anna, Noelle, Adrian, Isis, Kira, Alice—and their parents, who permitted me to photograph them. Additional kudos to the amazing people who administer the school, including Tonya Porter, Elizabeth Osei, and Nicole Kunz.

Library of Congress Control Number: 2006926898

ISBN 978-0-8109-1381-3

Image Permissions

Pages 4–5: ® The New York Public Library, Astor, Lenox and Tilden Foundations. Pages 18–19: "9," by Ivan Chermayeff, reprinted courtesy of Ivan Chermayeff/Chermayeff and Geismar; fountain courtesy of Fisher Brothers; "Love," by Robert Indiana, © 2006 Morgan Art Foundation Ltd./Artists Rights Society (ARS), New York; "Mahatma Gandhi," by Kanitel B. Patel, 1986, Union Square Park, courtesy of Collection of the City of New York/Parks & Recreation; "Life Undergound," by Tom Otterness © Tom Otterness, 14th Street–Eighth Avenue, A, C, E, L lines, New York, NY, commissioned and owned by Metropolitan Transportation Authority Arts for Transit, courtesy of Tom Otterness, Marlborough Gallery, and MTA Arts for Transit; "Alice in Wonderland," by Jose De Creeft, 1959, Central Park, courtesy of Collection of the City of New York/Parks & Recreation; "Tisch Children's Zoo Gate," by Paul Manship, 1961, Central Park, courtesy of Collection of the City of New York/Parks & Recreation; "Asia," by Daniel Chester French, courtesy of U.S. General Services Administration Public Buildings Service, Fine Arts Collection; "Red Cube," by Isamu Noguchi, © 2006 The Isamu Noguchi Foundation and Garden Museum, New York/Artists Rights Society (ARS), New York.

Book design by Chad W. Beckerman

Published in 2007 by Abrams Books for Young Readers, an imprint of ABRAMS. All rights reserved. No portion of this book may be reproduced, stored in a retrieval system, or transmitted in any form or by any means, mechanical, electronic, photocopying, recording, or otherwise, without written permission from the publisher.

Printed and bound in China
15 14 13 12 11 10 9 8 7

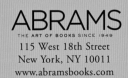

ABRAMS
THE ART OF BOOKS SINCE 1949
115 West 18th Street
New York, NY 10011
www.abramsbooks.com